Performance Peace

Written By: D.B. Guillory

Editors: Elizabeth Chereb and Eva Xan

Cover Illustration: Lilly Cole

Library of Congress Cataloging-in-Publication Data

Name: D.B. Guillory

Title: Performance Peace

ISBN: 978-1-66785-236-2

Subjects: Poetry / Spoken Word

Printed in the United States

Acknowledgements

A most humble "Thank You" to almighty God for his continued blessings. Even when I did not deserve it, you've showered me with your love, grace, and mercy. For that reason alone, I dedicate my life to do your will.

I also want to thank the Houston poetry scene for their love and support. I arrived as a stranger and was immediately loved like family. Your open arms have been my fortress of solitude.

Another thank you to every person that inspired the words you are about to read. You proved to be worthy of my time and attention, and I was compelled to write the story.

Finally, I want to thank all of my loved ones and frontline supporters. Without you, there would be no me. You encouraged me to step out into the unknown, and I am forever grateful for your presence in my life. I pray I can make you proud one day…

Table of Contents

Performance Peace

ACT I: Growth

Kingdom Man

Though my riches consist of intangibles,
I have peace of mind
In time my pieces shall increase,

Making way for glory and days of more
Brings waves of God's favor.
For my savior has prepared a table of good eats for me to savor.

Sit, and eat of my body
Drink of my blood
Do this in remembrance

For it is in my memory,
My mind, body, and soul
That the covenant I shall have and to hold, until,

I sing praises to the Most High
Even though my praises are off-key,
I see

His words are confirmation and all he asks is for obedience and dedication.
"Claim thee as thy Lord and Savior," he proclaims
I claim thee as my personal provider.
I claim thy word as my only decider.

Although I stumble and fall,
I know I can still crawl to you, and you lift me
You will always be with me.
I live to glorify you, and you in return, live within me.

Molded from dust into a perfect likeness and image
And to dust I shall return once this life has ended
But, my spirit will live on in the Kingdom.

In the Kingdom, I shall prep in God's Army
For when the day of reckoning is upon thee.
I will stand behind the word of the Lord, in one accord
Synchronized to perfection.

Because when the smoke clears,
My eternity will be eternally blissful.
And the abundance of milk and honey,
I will consume by the fistful.

P(i)eace

I'm just trying to gain a peace of mind,
These leeches just want a piece of mine.
I can't stay here to frame a piece of time.
God's got a plan of peace in due time.

But not now, not in this moment.
My time to shine is drowned out by the screams of false prophets,
Atheist schemes contradict the most definitely higher power.
The cowards prowess is subpar at best,
But we keep feeding the beast the Lord's flesh.

Forgotten how to bow with bended knees,
Expecting a favor over a blessing to precede any faithful actions.
Power-drunk followers, "What about me?!?!"
Echoes off the church walls from the outside.
Conviction is too painful to live on the inside.

Scared to follow blindly
Won't even ask, "Where are we going?," kindly.
"Jesus take the wheel" is something only accepted on the face of a meme,
Taking these clowns words as gospel.

Faithfully reading the posts verse for verse,
Quoting fear curse for curse.
Every third of my spoken word
Sees another verse to curse.

Like a business plan that won't let you escape the oppressions might,
Handouts and freebies won't bring you closer to the light.
Your spirit isn't bothered and that bothers me.
Your movements are unintelligent, and your thoughts are far from free

Your forked tongues tickle the bottom of my heel.
I have no urge to chuckle,
I press on.

The pressure won't make me buckle.
I know you're trying to have it your way in this space
Because you know that deep down,
You won't have a place in the Inn, and in the end you won't see His face.
You wasted too many prayers trying to keep up the pace.

Listen, the Joneses are living a different life.
The blessings they received came from a different height.
See all the hype got you all hyped up,
But when it comes to God you can't even get hyped up.

Unmotivated to use the blueprint to strengthen the wheel,
Won't consider the key to unlock your treasure you just rather steal,
All the resources are at your disposal,
It just doesn't really mix well with your seedy indecent proposals.

Just know that, God's got a plan of peace in due time.
I'll steer clear of the ones who leech for a piece of mine.
Because of my peace of mind,
I can't stay here.

Early Thirty

Up for no reason,
Staring at the shadows on these four walls,
Praying for all that I believe in,
Allowing the reality of this thing to sink in.

I was just thinking
About the different roads ahead of me,
Avoiding soft sand
S
  I
    N
      K
        I
          N
            G
Deeper into thought,
I just thought.

It all made sense
Until the two cents I was given
Became a nuisance to the rhythm.

The new sense was only the common sense I was missing.
So now I have a new reason, and a new season.
Still praying for all that I believe in.

I'm still thinking
Though
Getting to the end game requires conquering a few obstacles.

As long as my focus
Stays focused on my Godly course,
I'll be fine of course.

Just enjoy the journey
It's amazing the simple wisdom that reigns over you at....
Early thirty in the morning

When I Go

When I go,
I want to be dreaming
Having my family stand over me
Speak about how handsome I am
That I look like I'm sleeping.

I am!
Tired out from the good fight.
God and I spoke last night
About all my good nights.

God said,
"You made it harder than it had to be,
But my unconditional love you still got to see"
"Now gather yourself. You can't bring those belongings. Follow me."

We made a farewell lap around the places I'd been
Shared one last story about remembering when
I smiled in delight as we made the block.
Suddenly the atmosphere changed with a sudden stop.

God: "Did you do unto others as you would have them do unto you?"
Me: "I did my best, but my flesh won out more times than a few."

My spirit became convicted in that final moment.
I trembled in fear before my final judgment.
Had I done enough?
Did I leave this world better than I had found it?

God cracked a smile.....
"Yes, your acts were exceptional and your legacy astounding."
"You are perfectly imperfect, The Kingdom awaits"

Now I finally get to see my Poppa and sister at the gate.......

Act II: Intellect

Stay Woke

Many clowns around here yelling out "stay woke",
Prancing around my timeline with their balloons of hope,
Typing out real messages as tongue-and-cheek notes.

I got one too…
If you don't pay attention,
We are all going to float,
But what do I know?

I take naps.

Dreaming of the day when the mediocres present the facts
Instead of misinformation and misinterpretations,
Brainwashing the masses,
Manipulating the narrative before the whole story passes.

Yanking at your heartstrings
With images of a crying baby, standing in the shadow of an AR-15.
Just pan back a little,
The entire picture becomes painfully clear.

Not every blue blood yielding a glock deserves to be feared.
Yes!!!
There are a few that need to be diagnosed…

And I vividly remember a time when I wasn't supposed to live beyond 18,
And at most, 21,
But I did both.
Am I the exception to the rule?
Did the rule change?

Why is fear winning the click wars?
Or is the need to win the click wars to blame?
What does the winner of the click wars get?

A shiny statuesque man and bragging rights to fit?
The people are the losers in all of it.
But what do I know?
I take naps.

Dreaming of the day the mediocres present the facts,
Not feelings, not emotions, not forcing me to accept your truth,
But allowing me the freedom afforded to me to disagree, respectfully.

Instead of calling me a racist with phobias and "-isms"
Call me a man with a differing insightful opinion.

Free will of thoughts and actions is my God given right.
Staying woke doesn't mean I'm willing to bear arms in this mythical fight
How are my people supposed to take flight
When the fuel for our engines is spiked with spite?

Confusion is the compass navigating the steps.
Deception is the weight that we lift for our reps.

So don't clown around here yelling out "stay woke",
Knowing the substance in your balloons won't help my folks
Prancing around my timeline knowing your hope is a joke.

How about I give you a penny for the wise…
It's about time to float.
Stay Woke!

Charged

These cats are reciting lines like they're starting a revolution.
Pay attention to the cycle;
It's a vicious evolution.
Violence and hate dilutes the desired conclusion.
You've brought war to the streets, and it hasn't changed the constitution.

The dream that once was is slipping.
Now, it's more of an illusion.
All the nonsense makes no sense.
Quite frankly, it's a little confusing.

The goal was to make a political statement.
Instead, it became amusing.
What can be accomplished by all the rioting and the looting?

By the way, you destroyed your home, and in effect, your institution.
We have brains, and in them, wisdom equals a more productive solution.

But the reality is set in facts, and the decisions that were made in the aftermath
Has brought war to the streets, and the blood you seek.
All the fist pumps and feet pounds only accomplished cracks in the bricks.
I feel sick

To see people crumble a city.
You speak silently with your hands up, walk softly that path is very sticky.

Ignorance is still bliss.
Ignorant actions will not be dismissed.

We can't expect respect if we don't make the connection
Between a correct response and an immature reaction.
We want their face against our fist and their body beneath our feet.
Taking it by force won't return power to this scene.

The justice we seek and equality we speak has to start in our own community.
I charge ALL with the right and responsibility of accountability.
We can't fault other's actions, only our own.
Insure the homestead instead of moving along.

Ground zero is not the scene of the crime.
It's the birthplace of lessons.
If that time was missed, then stand up and make that confession.
It's not too late to instill values in the next generation
Help the youth reach beyond the desired destination.

Because if we don't, then society will raise our seeds.
Their way of life only instills greed.

The sad part is many of us treat this like a movie.
Society has glorified the ideals of a revolution,
Posting the preambles on facebook and other sources of social approval.

If you want to know the truth
They won't have to put us back in chains.
We are helping in that aspect.
We shackle ourselves with senseless acts and no gains.

The game is more complex and evolving every day.
We're on a chess board with checker pieces asking if we can play.

Wake up and pay attention!
We are behaving like the animals they once called us.

Since we demand the rights of a human being,
Display the intellectual characteristics of a sensible human being.

I charge myself and ALL with ownership of this constant maturation.
Unclench your fists and use your brain for emancipation!

Unspoken Tones

I speak silently and carry a big stick.
There are things I won't speak because they won't stick.
Open mouths and closed minds don't mix.
Every time I open my mind, and close my mouth I stack sense.

Common even, and even when the common is given.
Its strolled over like the comma I just rolled over
In the middle of this sentence.
It's senseless, the amount of attention paid to the pretentious.

Fed lies and corruption.
Well prepped line of destruction.
Little faith in the right, and the left is full of seduction.
Forever at war with the demonic faction,
Blinded by the glittery platinum distractions.

Make another beat
Provoking another beef.
Create another vine.
Try another challenge just to fill up the timelines.
For Christ's sake, pay attention to the actions!

Caught in between are the righteous, the innocent, the pious.
Tempted by the flesh of the beautiful liars
Turned away from the prophets trying to get higher.
Surviving in the sea of deceit
And constantly being asked, "So, what do you desire?"

The grand scheme of it all is to lead you astray
To keep you separated from the truth
And your god whenever you start to pray.
When you pray for the calm,
Then you become the prey.
When the predators catch wind of the truth that you were commissioned to say,
It's chaos!

That's the only way they know how to thrive
Destroying everything you believe; everything you love
Hoping you turn away from the noble life.

Some of us fall victim to this world dismissing the promise.
We refuse to lead each other back to the affiance.
We encourage outrage and outright defiance
And wonder why we can't get ahead with our alliance.

Trust me, I tried it...
I was convicted
Faced with the decision some believed to be hard to live with
Stand alone for a purpose, or in the crowd with misfits.
I chose the former, and my peace is now endless.
I'm an outcast in this world,
I'm just fine with it.

You're welcome to tag-a-long if it's truth that you seek...
See what I mean about the things I won't speak?
Just because my lips don't part it doesn't make me weak.
It doesn't make me a coward, and won't let me sleep.
I dwell well in my castle.
I rest well in my home.
This is just a snowflake on the iceberg of..........Unspoken Tones.

Act III: Family Ties

My Hero

Hulk Hogan body-slammed Andre The Giant, and I went ballistic
I ran around the house and my parents were like, "What is this?"
I said "It's Hulka-mania brother, it's just that serious!"
He was my hero.
Until I grew older and colder to the staged presence I came to know.
Plus, it really pissed me off when he became a member of N.W.O.
He was my hero.

I ripped a few undershirts trying to match his strength.
Somewhere around that time I knew I could leap tall buildings
In a single bound like my hero Clark Kent
I mean Khal-El, the son of Jor-El from the planet of Krypton.
Standing for everything pure and he could endure anything and destroy anyone.
He was kind hearted with a soft side for Ms. Lane.
He made time reverse so he could try to save her again.
He was my hero.

With breath as cold as ice, and eyes that burned right through you of course,
My hero became paralyzed when he fell off that horse,
And all I could say was "Damn!"
Not Superman, not Kal-El, not the son of Jor-El…

Now my heros were just a shell of their former selves;
I couldn't believe it.
I'm older now and looking back on those days,
I realize the fault in my praise
My heros were men who played characters to get paid,
But, I had one last hero that was too real to be that fake.

He stands about 5'8" with a calming disposition.
Quick to write you off if you come around here with an nonessential inquisition
Take aim at his unit, and he'll pop a few in your direction
He's 73 yrs old, and he ain't got time for your silliness with his blessings.
He's my hero.

He gave me life,
Body-slammed those giants and taught me how to fight.
Put your hands up like this, bob and weave.
Then, we had to stop when I slipped a jab and put a hook under his sleeve.
He's my hero.

He knocked down every tall building so I could thrive.
Taught me how to live instead of how to survive
He taught me to seek the truth, even when I'm surrounded by the lies.
When I was 14, he told me to be a good person
And instilled in me a never quit attitude.
The magnitude of my attitude can take me far.
My hero taught me how to spot an unclean spirit that would disrupt the cause.

My hero isn't perfect, and he's been broken beyond repair.
Every time he was counted out, his spirit wouldn't fight fair.
His strength was forged from the fires in the depths of his despair.
Tell me, how many of you would quit if your daughter died in her sleep,
And all you could do was sit there?

My hero was farther from his father than anyone could get.
My hero didn't bother and took the reins to see how farther he could get.

My hero.... broken, lost, and torn got up from his seat and chose to carry on.
He led us through without missing a beat.
Yeah he stumbled, he fumbled, but he never admitted defeat.

I watched my hero give his most valuable possession.....time.
My hero isn't rich, my hero isn't blind.
If he sees you doing right, he will be just as kind

There is a fine line between what he will accept.
There were plenty of times when my hero went and grabbed that belt.
The wisdom that flows from his mouth now sounds a little hypocritical

"Don't be hitting on them kids."
"Wait! You bruised me up for some of the things that I did."
"I was young. I thought I knew, but in the end I didn't even have a clue."

"If you can't talk to them they ain't worth nothing anyway.
That's the new lesson I have for you."
"Okay cool, but what about that time.....nevermind I deserved that too."

My hero taught me how to swing a bat,
And the memories we created became etched in stats.
We still have the newspaper clipping as a matter of fact.

I wanted desperately to grow up to be just like those characters I idolized
One day my hero told me
I'm living a life that he himself couldn't even prophesize.
"You're living *my* dream."
I was stunned because I know what he means
He wanted better for me so he made the sacrifices
And the fruits of his labor are ripe for the harvest.
My hero planted his faith deep in the word of God and endured the hardship.

Now, he reaps the benefits of a job well done.
I call my hero Daddy.
My hero calls me son.

Through it all, he's my hero today just as he was on day one.
My hero gave me everything I needed to get the job done.
I hope I bring honor to his name before God sets his sun.
Long live my hero in this life and beyond.

Legacy

You were born from my seed.
I watched you grow from an embryo
Into an itty bitty me.
The words you speak are so familiar to me.
The actions I see are like looking into "The Way Back"
And way back I acted the same,
So now when I hush you,
My own experiences begin to rush through.
Deep down I smile, but you would never know from my exterior growl.
I had to apologize to many, especially when I heard you open your mouth
And you didn't understand that your childish words were offending.
Continuously, I was reminded that some long time ago I had no filter either
Now I laugh out loud as your father.
I stand up proud of the person you've become.
Oh the many changes we've endured and the many battles we have won
Has brought us closer together than ever before,
Now I watch you walk into the world,
And I can't help but to stand and sob at the door.
That seed that came from me
Grew from an embryo into their own individual self sustaining being.

Voicemail

Makes a Phone Call

A lot has happened in the years gone by.
I matured enough to be acceptable and I even have kids, yeah what a surprise
A beautiful daughter and a handsome son,
Growing up to be better than their dad.
I try not to spoil them.
I just give them
Things we had.
A dad
That spent time and not money.
You would've loved their sense of humor
It's scary to see a mini me and a mini us.
I totally understand why mom told us not to fight
Why dad would grit his teeth when he cussed
It's funny how the world has changed, but no flying cars yet.
The only Jet I have is the sons on the TV.
Lol I know
Wow, it's been a while!
The last time I saw you, you were wearing that white dress surrounded by pink.
Quiet, motionless and I used to think....
Why did you run away from home?
Little did I know you were already there,
Playing with Poppa without a care.
By the way, when you see him, tell him I said, "Hi."
Let him know I'm doing just fine, in the years gone by.
Alright I gotta go, these people looking at me like I'm crazy as hell.
I love you and I miss you!
I just had to have this conversation on your voicemail…………..Cancer sucks!

Hey Momma!

Hey momma!
Remember when I fell in love with you
Before I even left your womb?
Sleeplessness, worried days, hard lessons coming soon

Hey momma!
Remember when you brought your baby boy home?
It was bittersweet for Nikki
She had to share her birthday.
She's still in her feels in the worst way
It's cool though.

Hey momma!
Remember when I used a permanent marker
to draw the road map to a butt-whooping on your bamboo wallpaper?
I remember it like last night
You made my left cheek, right cheek shine bright

Hey momma!
Remember all the times we danced in the kitchen?
The smile on your face was priceless.
My rhythm was a little off, but the timing was perfect.
You're the reason I dance with my sweetheart I'm certain.

Hey momma!
Remember that time you took me to the ER
Because that sewing needle broke off in my foot?
You held my hand when I thought the doctor would have to cut me to the bone.
Looking back, I was terrified, but you stayed by my side the whole time.

Hey momma!
Remember that time I didn't get my work done?
You told me to play my best game that day
Because it was going to be the last one of the season.
I remember we won.

I played like I would never play again
Hey daddy!
You should've let momma bench me
No pass!
She ain't playing.

Hey momma!
Remember when I was in college?
I took the money you gave me for gas and groceries,
And used it to see Erykah Badu in Fort Worth
Yeah, that trip was fun and the fact you didn't trip was surprising.
At least I told the truth and you told me not pull that "S" again

Hey momma!
Remember when my heart was broken?
You stepped in and mended it back together.
I knew I would love you forever.
I knew then the same thing I know now

Your scent will always be home,
Your hugs will be my salvation,
Your smile will cover my spirit,
Your heartbeat will be my calm in the storm.

Hey momma!
When I was face down in a tailspin and didn't know what to do
You listened and I figured it out.
I stopped crying, and it's hell to pay, right?

Hey momma!
I know you aren't perfect, but you are perfect for me
You have been everything I needed and more.

Hey momma!
Thank you for raising your hand
So you could help raise a man.

Hey momma!
I see your strength,
Especially the way you love after heartbreak.
Remember when you coaxed a 5 year old me off the back steps after the
funeral?
 LVH

Hey momma!
I remember the good, the bad, and the funny.
You talk smack with the best of them.
Can you still lift your leg high enough to kick my butt?

Hey momma!
I am forever grateful for every memory

Hey momma!
I love you!

How Much I Love You
Written by: Lady Elyse (My Sweetheart)

You touch my soul with your love for me
and your spirit fills my heart with joy,
but when we depart, you always
find a way to keep me in your arms.
So, I tell you now how much I love you.

Act IV: I Love You?

Decent Proposal

A young Queen of Queens moved far from her sea. To refresh her perspective on where her life may lead. Her focus is so focused it's bursting at the seams, but she is still focused nonetheless on a mission to succeed. Meanwhile, a class act character is moving amongst the clouds creating a scene. Doing his best to solidify his future using blessings and favors to reach his dreams. Giving his focus to rebuilding and cultivating all that he needs, but his focus is only focused enough to allow him room to see. So then, walks in, this Queen of Queens. The class act character stammers a bit, but regains his steam. "Speak clearly," he thinks, "and don't say anything crazy or mean. Be gentle, but firm; clever and not silly; being yourself is the best thing." He listens closely to her words, keeping his thoughts very keen. So, he must respect the position of that Queen of Queens. As time ticks on he prepares for the unseen, but before he carried forward he chose these words to speak.

Excuse me Miss, but I believe that belongs to me. I am speaking of the attention you began to receive. It's no mistaking the perception of the interest and how genuine it must be. So let me clarify how close this venture might seem. I don't need anything more than a glimpse or a gleam. A glance would do just fine as long as I have the chance to be. I would like for it to be more than a solitary me. However, I understand the timing may not be conducive to nurturing a realistic we. I have to be honest because I know that loose lips sink ships, and closed mouths don't feed. So I'll speak the words to be heard whether in success or defeat. Will you do me the honor of considering to be. A closer friend than before and give me the chance to believe. That my eyes are not clouded and my thoughts are not false, and you are that Queen that I believe you to be in my heart? To which she replied: "I'm seeing somebody."

28

Just Sayin'

Real love though,
It can't find its way to the surface
Cats breathing life into this fake love flow.
Standing wide-eyed in front of the truth
Can't comprehend the totality of a genuine true folk,
So why are you entertaining these prosthetic people posing as true love, yo?
Oh, my bad
I didn't realize you were walking around with both eyes closed.
Spending their time unfaithful to the most.
No credit in the quality
That's why they're always broke.
As you journey down Lazy Love River,
You'll soon find out you're up Schitt's Creek without a paddle or a boat
Stranded outside Lover's Cabin in the middle of the winter without a coat
I hope,
You see the light before the darkness strangles the growth.
All I'm really asking is
What do you deserve?
Through this strange love note

If I Say

If I say that I miss you,
Would you hold it against me?
If I say that I need you
Would you bleed your heart within me?
If I say that you complete my sentence, period
Would you dramatically end it?
If I say that you are the mark of my question,
Would you be offended?
If I say that I would gladly take your frown if you did not smile,
If I say that I would happily stand beside you beaming with pride,
If I say that I would capture every moment and pin it in the sky,
Would you still be willing to just pass me by?
If I say that I'll squeeze you tight when it thunders,
Would you look past my many faults and my many blunders?
If I say that I can ease your tearful fears,
Would you take a chance to gain blissful years?
If I say that nothing can keep me from you,
Would you roadblock my advances to shun me from you?
If I say that I will give you my spirit,
Would you become callous and indifferent?
If I say that nothing matters at this moment,
If I say that your whole being is my fortress,
If I say that you are my last breath,
And you knew I was dying, I would still say keep that for yourself.
If I say I'm good with my life because you were in it,
Would you know how much love I had invested in it?
If my last will and testament was to see your face.
Would you finally understand how much love I gave in this place?
But if I say nothing,
You would not know to answer

A Snippet

A tease of a piece of a whole,
Meant to attract the attention of the soul.
A part of a section of the entirety
Capturing the consideration in its entirety.
A place in the background of a place you crave back now.
An alluring scene that won't, back down.
At bay and more than arm's length,
Deliberating the facts with just a small "ength".
Fragmented platelets shedding from a fast-paced case list,
Handing you a full glass and making a request for you to just taste this.
It's not fair!
I don't care for a keepsake.
I'll gladly take a snippet,
But I would rather experience the full-scale of the rhythm of the beat your heart
makes.

Captivated

You consume my thoughts with reckless disregard,
A concoction of hopeful hopelessness
A chemical imbalance sure to debilitate
You are charismatic and contagious
Even at high noon my subconscious dreams of things so sweet.
There is an ever present bitter tingle
My sights are set to seek out the possibility
The probability of the likelihood carries chances and odds
Oddly enough, the belief is still far fetched
You are within a stretch of a fingertip
And might as well be arms length away
Just a few steps to enter your space
And those might as well be miles of squares to cover.
My heart flutters yes, but it doesn't break pace,
Who am I kidding it's jumping in my chest with every part of my lips
The pleasure you place on my vessels makes me fatigued
How do I muster enough, to make it enough, to be enough
How do I say enough, to reveal enough, to get enough
Easier said than done, just simplify the factors
A simple proposition, a declaration if you must
Madam, ma'am, miss, please amplify your presence within my soul.

Emotional Rock

When you're caught between an emotional rock and a hard place,
It could be a very surreal feel.
All the things you want felt
Have all but left.
And you stare deeply into the eyes of quality of life
And, how you're going to deal
With the future.

Unsure of the next move
Because your next move is a load bearing wall
And all the things you used to know
Seems to not know you at all.

You decide to keep the peace,
And the peace you seek
It's just a bandage on the wound.
Not healed and unfulfilled,
There is still tension in the room.

A glimpse of normalcy and how it used to be
Makes you wonder
Whether or not moving on is a step that needs to be taken,
Knowing all the while you're just going through the motions
Pretending smiling, smirking, and faking.

When you're caught between an emotional rock and a hard place,
Things get real very quick.
Your reflection flashes before you
And your reflection time becomes a chambered existence.
The many decisions that are before you cause much resistance.
And in the distance
Is the inevitable

An unwavering forecast of hell-bent maneuvers,
Answers seem to be far away with unexpected solutions.

Amongst the confusion a moment of clarity stares back
And you'll see that
Any move you make will break you.

So no moves are made, and you try to blank out your thoughts,
Only to be left with an empty feeling in your chest
And a hole in your heart.

You've seen this situation before and have taken some missteps
And have made some mistakes.
Painful is the love that is caught between an emotional rock and a hard place.

Debra's Ode

I see my happiness in your eyes
Glaring passed your past to see where my future lies
Your heart is my temple, that's where my peace resides
Journey's fate took its sweet time to come around the bend, and then I realize,
That your beauty is far beyond skin deep
It's so thick
I'm stuck in it
So vast
I'm lost in it
So sensual
I create love, and love is created with it
So valuable
I'll cross a barren desert just to rediscover it
So intoxicating
I'm addicted to it
Inject every vein
Make me feen for it
Lifts me high
So I can fly with it
Infect my heart, keep that cure
I'll just die with it
I see my happiness in your eyes
Glaring passed my past to see where my future lies
Your heart is my temple, that's where hate is denied
Journey's fate took its sweet time and brought us back around to Freedom's
field just for me to realize, that your soul extends beyond the constellations
It's my sanctuary
I'll pray in it
My shelter from the storm
Blessed to be covered with it
Comfort in my time of need and my needs are caressed within it
A place to rest my head
I'll just lay in it
Conquer all of my fears
I'll just slay with it

You've always had my back
And the days I've fallen you've helped me stand with it
That's why I see my future in your life
No turning back now
No back downs
Here's your crown
Set aside the pride
Help me rule this kingdom, with an open mind, and decisive tone
I'm humbled in this moment
This is Debra's Ode.
I'll give you all my riches
You deserve your highness role
The first 38 made you great
Now we're living in thriving mode
Shed a tear, it's okay.
Every drop has thank you as an undertone
My heart is your home
Your happy place
I'll take you to the waves
All smiley faced
I see my future in your life
As I glare into those eyes
Looking passed my past to see what the future holds
What a sweet embrace to behold
An enchanted story to be told
All I know is,
I'm humbled in this moment
I'm in love
And this is Debra's Ode

Untitled (Love)

You know I still love you right?
Like more than a friend, but less than a wife.
I added that in to make it more realistic like
Like more than yesterday, but less than tomorrow's plight.

Sometimes I dream of making that phone call
Saying, "Hey! What you doing for the next three days and nights?"
"Nothing!!! Cool!!!"
"Pack your bags 'cause I found a connecting flight."

With no questions asked we put aside all that fright
So don't fret my friend
We'll be back to our regular selves after the light sheds thrice
Looking around trying to build up the might
To say "What the hell is happening?" while we sway in the moonlight.

I know this is just a fantasy conjured up for my subconscious delight,
But that is the only time I get to stare at those eyes
The only time I hug you and squeeze you tight,
Never letting loose the grips of your lips,
Knowing all this is just in spite of
Listening to every word with pause and excite.

Smiling in content cause my soul is like
You know I still love you right?
Like more than a friend.....

Act V: Packing Up

Later

I'm sorry you don't feel the same,
I can't find the words to explain why my actions changed,
Maybe because the love I have for you is locked in a choke hold
And I'm afraid that if I ease up just a little
You'd see something different and I'll be something different
Basically, my heart just can't find that control
I've closed the door plenty times before
But this time I'll leave that key
Under the Welcome Back mat that rests quietly at the back door
I understand that right now less has to be more and what more can I say
I want more, but the more I pull it just pushes you away
And every time I see a glimpse of your face
My heart wants to scream out "WAIT!!!"
Don't go, please just stay
But I know that you must venture on
Regardless of how brightly my smile shines when you turn me on
And, so on
The next time we meet
I hope the words we speak leaves us in place of truth and acceptance
I'll do my best with a deep breath
Not to invade your personal space with unwelcome transgressions
I pray this is for the best
And I pray the Lord will order our steps in the way we should go
Just know
That you are my first thought at day break
And my last thought after I count that last sheep
There are no words to describe how I feel at this moment
I just know that this love and your absences cuts me mad deep
Later…

Fantastic Lies

Say what you feel, it's all the same to me.
You've laid it all out,
And your actions show something different than who you claim to be.
It made sense for a minute, until I began to see,
No longer bound by the ties created by your falsies.

I was held hostage by the strength of your mouthpiece.
Spit game.
Damn shame that your superhero power was used to misguide and deceive.
"It is what it is"
Is what I was made to believe.
But now I know that *it* was never compared to what *is* was sold to be.
It got old to me.

All I have now are these fleeting memories.
I don't lose sleep much anymore.
I don't expect to see your silhouette at the door.
I just breathe
On my knees, every morning praying that God provides the strength I need
To move beyond the sense of this scene.
And so far He has heard me.
So, say what you feel, it's all the same to me.
You've laid it all out, and now you get the cold-shoulder breeze.
It all made sense for a minute until I began to see
No longer bound by the lies.

Now all I have to do is just *be*
Spit game.
Damn shame that it had to be something it was never meant to be.
But *it* will never compare to the truth
And the truth won't be sold short of what the truth is supposed to be.

Welcome to Your New Life

Welcome to your new life
Tell me how does it look?
When you grabbed that pen,
Did you have a title for this book
It appears the chapters
Are full of many have to's
Many of the lines focus on the hereafter.
So what are you here after?
The answers you seek
Seem to be rooted very deep.
You can't uproot without kicking around some dirt.
Yes, it will hurt.
You flirt with the end,
And in the end, losses are great and vast.
Before long, a new cast full of a variety of characters
Will be subjected to verses of curses, half truths and bold-face lies.
Even the harmless little whites...... will blacken your eye.
When you grabbed that pen,
Did you have a title for this book?
Now look, a few gentle words is all it took.
But the words never came, it's a shame.
It's definitely not the same
All aboard the change train!
Next stop is the next stop, but it won't be the last.
Wherever that may be, may He be with thee.
That pen should be inked to the brim,
And make sure that title is glorifying Him.

Act VI: Where's the Poetic Value?

Jabber

Have you ever wondered what happens when your hamster falls on the wheel and gets trapped? Me too! That's why I gave mine a Life Alert *(Help I've fallen and I can't get up...)* Cycle and recycle, and the cycle continues on and on and on and on and... Man I'm so tired and it feels like a run-on (so on and so on). So far, I have accomplished nothing except for that one time when I finally completed that task on that day so many months ago. That felt good. I breathed a sigh of relief and then, I remembered that I needed to go to the store to pick something up, but then I couldn't remember so I just sat there staring at the walls with the TV on for background noise. I dozed off and right before my chin touched my chest, I woke and yelled "toilet paper". Yes, toilet paper is what I needed from the store. So, I hopped in my truck and I took off. Then the dilemma became," well what store?"

Eighth Grade Awkward

It would behoove me to know
Whether or not Roses could show
The likeness I have for you.

Please check yes or no.
I'm just eighth grade awkward.

It would satisfy an urge
To express every single verb
With the adjective that is you.

Please check yes or no.
I'm just eighth grade awkward.

How about a kind word
Or some random act of kindness?
Surely you will see beyond the blinders

Please check yes or no.
I'm just eighth grade awkward.

Please let me know
If you would like to go
Anywhere with me.

Please check yes or no.
I'm just 8th grade awkward.

In my final attempt,
I spill my feelings and then
You will check yes or no.
I'm just 8th grade awkward.

Placed Words

A few well placed words can go a long way
Like, are my, after, you, and before, world
The arrangement lends credit to something far more precious
And it's meaning is incredibly powerful

A few well placed words can carry a message beyond comparison
Like, my heart, finishing the beginning of, you're, and after, smile melts
The alignment of such vocabulary breathes life
And it's meaning is incredibly powerful

A few well placed words can boast of things so grand
Like, to be my, before, last time falling, after, I want my first sight of you, and
close with, in love.
Unexplainable are the effects of such verbiage
And it's meaning is incredibly powerful

A few well placed words can......

If The Shoe Fits

Stretched out and full of it,
Kept close and tried a bit.
It's high time for a new set,
And I bet you have no clue on the size to get.
I've had my heels stomped on and mashed down,
Cleaned up and wash down,
Tied up right and wound up tightly.
Had my strings pulled many times then stored away nightly.
Worn out and scuffed up,
Reconditioned for the reconstruct.
My tongue hangs low because my soul is torn more.
The design of the makeup is important to the shakeup.
Describe it how you want and provide whatever explanation you think fits.
I'll wear it, but only if the shoe fits.

Remembered

I wanted to be remembered for something greater than myself.
Selfless on the surface,
Selfish beneath these lines.
The truth piercing hidden lies behind my eyes.
I just wanted to be remembered.
I guess I should have just remembered
Why…

LATER.........